# High-Interest READING

by
**Renee Cummings**

**Cover Design by**
**Matthew Van Zomeren**

**Inside Illustrations by**
**Rebecca Waske**

*Publisher*
Instructional Fair • TS Denison
Grand Rapids, Michigan 49544

## Permission to Reproduce

Instructional Fair • TS Denison grants the right to the individual purchaser to reproduce the student activity materials in this book for noncommercial, individual, or classroom use only. Reproduction for an entire school or school system is strictly prohibited. No part of this publication may be reproduced for storage in a retrieval system, or transmitted in any form or by any means, electronic, mechanical, recording, or otherwise, without the prior written permission of the publisher. For information regarding permission write to: Instructional Fair • TS Denison, P.O. Box 1650, Grand Rapids, MI 49501.

## About the Author

**Renee Cummings** is an experienced author, having written numerous books for Instructional Fair. She holds a Bachelor's Degree in Elementary Education from Oregon State University. Her 18 years of experience in the classroom include teaching various elementary levels and remedial reading. Renee resides in Hood River, Oregon, with her husband, who currently presides as the town's mayor.

## Credits

Author: Renee Cummings
Cover Design: Matthew Van Zomeren
Inside Illustrations: Rebecca Waske
Project Director/Editor: Sharon Kirkwood
Editors: Eunice Kuiper, Wendy Letts
Typesetting/Layout: Pat Geasler

# Table of Contents

**Answer Key (in middle of book)**

# A Sparkling Crop

A farmer in Arkansas couldn't understand why crops would grow only on part of his land. Then, one day he found two tiny crystals. A jeweler told him the crystals were diamonds! The part of his land that would not grow crops was sitting over a diamond mine.

About twenty-five years ago this land was turned into the Crater of Diamonds State Park. Many people go there every year to hunt for diamonds. Any diamonds people find are theirs to keep! Doesn't this sound like a great place to go for an exciting vacation?

Follow the directions.

1.  Draw a barn in the middle of the space to the left of the farmer.

2.  Draw a  in the middle of the space to the right of the farmer. Write **Crater of Diamonds** on the sign.

3.  Draw 4 corn stalks in the left corner above the barn.

4.  Draw 6 pumpkins in the left corner below the barn.

5.  Below the sign draw a large rock with 6 diamonds on it.

6.  Above the sign draw you holding 2 diamonds in one hand and 4 diamonds in the other hand.

# To the Docks

The wind blew. Waves splashed over the sides of the fishing boat. We sat inside the small cabin and watched as Captain Caitlin held a tight grip on the helm. He peered at the stormy sea. There was only darkness. Captain Caitlin blinked every time a wave smashed against the window. He kept searching for any sign of land.

"There it is!" he shouted. We stretched our necks to peek out the window. A tiny light beamed in the distance.

Captain Caitlin steered carefully past the rocky cliffs. Then he turned right to sail the boat through the opening that led to the dock. Everyone sighed as the boat gently bumped against the dock and stopped moving. We all clapped as Captain Caitlin tied the boat to the dock.

Follow the directions to help Captain Caitlin steer his boat to safety at the dock. Draw a line from the boat to show where each direction leads Captain Caitlin.

1. Sail south to the two rocks.

2. Go east between the two rocks.

3. Steer north under the bridge.

4. Continue northwest to the Coast Guard Station.

5. Head north again to the Fishing Trips Office.

6. Slow the engines and go south toward the dock.

7. Go to slot C. Draw a picture of the boat.

# Night Sounds

After a busy day, nighttime seems so quiet. There are fewer cars. Fewer people are outside, too.

But listen! It really isn't as quiet as it seems. A breeze passes through a tree's branches. There is a gentle rustle as the leaves flutter.

A tiny tree frog makes a croaking sound. It stops and waits for an answer. Another croak is heard, only this time it is a little farther away.

The night is filled with singing, not by people, but by crickets. Rubbing their front wings together, they make a chirping sound—like music.

The next time you are sitting outside on your porch or in your yard, listen to the wonderful sounds that nature makes at night. These are soft and quiet sounds for you to enjoy.

The sentence on each moon tells something that happened. Find the sentence that tells why it happened and write the letter in the star on the tip of the moon.

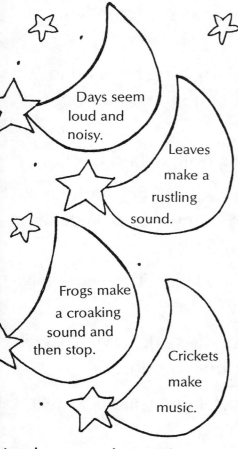

a. They are trying to find other frogs.

b. The wind blows through the branches.

c. They are rubbing their wings together.

d. There are lots of people and cars on the streets.

List the sounds you hear at night and tell what makes those sounds.

_____

_____

_____

# The Great Lace-Up Race

"Let's race!" said Cecil as he grabbed his sneakers.

"Okay," laughed Cindy.

"Ready, set, go!" they said, looking at each other. Quickly they each put on their first sneaker.

"Ha-ha!" said Cecil as he finished tying his second sneaker and was putting his foot into the third one. "I'm ahead of you!"

The seconds ticked away. "Oh, no!" sighed Cecil.

"Oops!" giggled Cindy. She saw that Cecil had the lace of sneaker twenty-one tied to the lace of sneaker twenty-two.

Cecil grumbled as he untied the laces. Then carefully he retied the sneakers correctly.

Soon Cindy stood up and proudly said, "I win!" Cecil was just finishing tying sneaker one hundred.

"Let's have another race," challenged Cindy. "Let's race to that big leaf on the pumpkin plant."

Away they scampered.

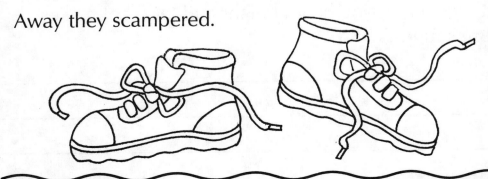

1.  Draw a picture of Cecil or Cindy.




2.  What clue(s) in the story tell you about Cecil
    and Cindy?

    _____

    _____

    _____

Circle the answer.

1.  What did Cecil and Cindy like to do?

    tease each other        race            tie their shoes

2.  How many races did they have in the story?

    one            two            three            four


Write about another race Cecil and Cindy could have.

_____

_____

_____

_____

# Kaboom!

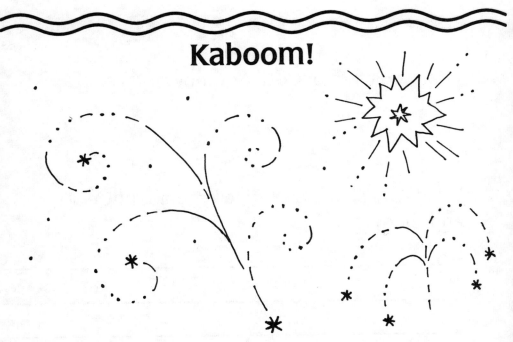

Kaboom! Everyone looks up. Pop! The sky is filled with tiny white sparkling lights. Pop! Now there are tiny twinkling blue lights. Pop! Pop! Little red stars begin falling from the sky.

If it had not been for a mistake made by a cook in China a very long time ago, we may not have these beautiful fireworks. He was using things that were found in all kitchens at the time, but he created an explosion that he didn't expect.

Shortly after the cook's explosive food, the Chinese put the ingredients in a hollow bamboo tube. When they lit it, the bamboo tube soared up into the sky. It exploded into small, bright, twinkling lights. These first fireworks were called "arrows of flying fire."

Follow the directions to make a beautiful fireworks display.

1. Connect the dots from *a* to *r* to make the shape of the fireworks.

2. Draw 5 yellow stars above the top point.

3. Draw 6 stripes on the top part of the fireworks. Color 3 stripes purple and 3 stripes orange.

4. Use three different colors to draw 9 wavy lines across the middle of the fireworks.

5. Color 2 of the flames orange and 3 of the flames red.

# Moose on the Loose

"What was that?" wondered Grady as he walked past the window. He turned and walked back to look outside. There were two very large things bobbing up and down. Grady nodded his head with the motion. At first it looked like gigantic hands reaching for the window.

Grady froze. Suddenly two big brown eyes appeared. It was a moose! Its mouth was moving from side to side. The moose blinked. Grady blinked.

Slowly Grady moved to the back door. He quietly opened the door and peeked out around the corner. Then the moose tilted its head and peeked back at Grady. They stared at each other. After a few moments, the moose just blinked and went back to eating Mom's flowers.

Read the clues. Find the correct word in the story and write it on the lines.

1. huge
   ___ ___ ___ ___ ___ ___ ___
                                                   1

2. stood very still
   ___ ___ ___ ___ ___
             2

3. part of the face
   ___ ___ ___ ___ ___
                 3  4

4. a forest animal
   ___ ___ ___ ___ ___
      5

5. type of plants ___ ___ ___ ___ ___ ___
             6                   7

6. opened and closed eyes
   ___ ___ ___ ___ ___ ___
             8

7. opposite of loudly
   ___ ___ ___ ___ ___ ___
       9

8. leaned
   ___ ___ ___ ___ ___ ___
    10              11

Use the numbered letters to find out why Mom was so surprised that the moose ate her flowers.

Didn't the moose know that they were

___ ___ ___ ___ ___ - ___ ___
10  2   9   1   4    5  11

___ ___ ___ ___?
8  6  3  7

# An Edible Car

Imagine you are riding in an edible car. Your stomach growls, so you snap off a radio knob for a snack. This can't be real!

The same man who made cars that almost everyone could afford to buy was also interested in people eating healthful food. He felt soybeans were the healthiest of all foods, so he used them in building cars. First, he started farms to grow soybeans. Then, he built processing plants to take the oil out of the soybeans. He used the soybean oil to make car parts. Some of the parts he made were horn buttons, switch handles, and control knobs. He dreamed about building an entire car using soybean oil. It never happened.

Of course, there were other ingredients used with the soybean oil, so it couldn't really be eaten. If you got hungry while out for a drive, you would still have to stop at a restaurant.

Read each sentence. Color the  gas gauge if it is a good idea. Color the  gas gauge if it is a bad idea.

  Someone should make cars that almost everyone can afford to buy.

  We should be able to eat car parts.

  Everyone should eat soybeans three times a day.

  Someone should find more uses for soybean oil.

 People should grow soybeans on every farm because there are so many uses for them.

Use food shapes to design an "edible" car. Label the foods.

# The Cookie-Napper

"Fresh-baked cookies are ready for tomorrow's picnic," said Mom to herself. She set the full cookie jar on the counter. Then she went to the attic to get the picnic basket and other things that would be needed.

Later, when she came back into the kitchen, she saw muddy fingerprints on the sides and lid of the cookie jar. Oh, no! Someone had already sampled tomorrow's treats. Mom grabbed a cloth to wipe off the prints. As she moved the jar, it felt very light. Being careful not to get her hands muddy, Mom lifted the lid. Someone had definitely been in the cookie jar. It was empty!

Who is the cookie-napper?

Solve the case. Find whose fingerprints
match the muddy prints
on the cookie jar.

Suspects in the cookie-napping are:

| Gloria | Hannah | Andy | Pete | Claire | Pedro |

Whose fingerprints are on the cookie jar?

_____

A little later the cookies reappeared. It was just a joke
played on Mom. What would be a fair punishment for
the crime of cookie-napping?

_____

_____

_____

_____

# Bump!

Bumpler! That's what everyone called him. He was always bumping into everything. Sometimes he even buzzed around the wrong hive.

Being very polite, he always said, "Excuse me. I'm sorry. I didn't see you." He would then fly away feeling very embarrassed.

Bump! "Oh, no," said Bumpler. Tears filled his eyes.

"It's okay. You didn't hurt me. My name is Dr. Beeline. Why don't you let me check your eyes?" buzzed the doctor.

It wasn't easy, but Bumpler followed the doctor to his office. After a few minutes, Dr. Beeline said, "All you need are some eyeglasses! Here, try these."

"Wow! I can see everything. Thank you!" said Bumpler as he buzzed out of the office.

Away he flew! He swerved right and left and never bumped into anything again.

Check the correct box to tell when the words best describe Bumpler.

| | Before meeting Dr. Beeline | After meeting Dr. Beeline |
|---|---|---|
| unhappy | | |
| confident | | |
| embarrassed | | |
| poor vision | | |
| good vision | | |
| happy | | |
| clumsy | | |
| avoided things | | |
| liked buzzing around | | |

What name do you think his friends called him now?

_____

Draw a picture of how
Bumpler looks and feels
at the end of the story.

# A Great Wall

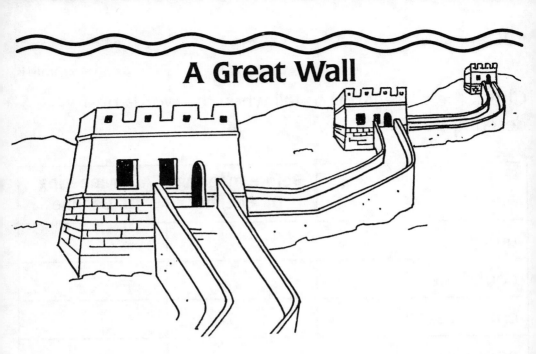

Imagine you are on a space shuttle. You look out the window at the earth. If you look very closely, you can see a thin line across China. This is the Great Wall of China.

Thousands of people worked hundreds of years to build this wall. It was needed to protect China from its enemies to the north.

Parts of the Great Wall have crumbled. Some parts have been repaired. It is of great interest to scientists and historians who study the wall. One company has special permission to collect loose pebbles from the Great Wall and sell them to visitors. What a great opportunity to get a piece of history!

The Great Wall is no longer needed to keep enemies out. Instead it has become a great tourist attraction for visitors to China.

Unscramble the letters and write the missing words on the lines.

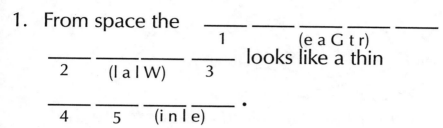

1. From space the ___ ___ ___ ___ ___
   1   (e a G t r)
   ___ ___ ___ ___ looks like a thin
   2   (l a l W)   3

   ___ ___ ___ ___ .
   4   5   (i n l e)

2. It is in northern ___ ___ ___ ___ ___ .
   (a n C i h)   6

3. It was built to ___ ___ ___ ___ ___ ___
   7   (t e p o r c t)   8
   China from its enemies.

4. It took ___ ___ ___ ___ ___ ___ ___
   9   (e h r u d n d s)   10   11
   of years for the people to build the wall.

5. Only one ___ ___ ___ ___ ___ ___ ___
   (m c o p n a y)   12
   can sell pebbles from parts of the wall that have
   crumbled.

Use the numbered letters to "build" the coded message.

___ ___   ___ ___   ___
 5   8     5   11    6

___ ___ ___ ___ ___
 8   7   9   3   12

" ___ ___ ___ ___ ___ " ___ ___ ___ ___ !
   1   7   10   6   8     2   6   3   3

# Perfectly Named Animal

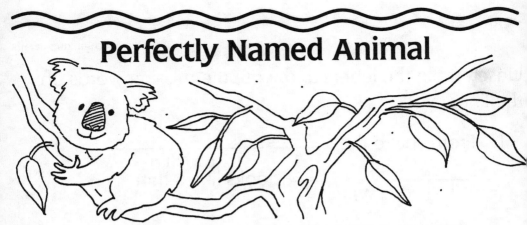

Cute and cuddly are two words that describe the Australian koala. Its soft, thick, gray fur, round ears, and stubby tail make it a lovable animal.

It has been called bangaroo, koolewong, narnagoon, buidelbeer, native bear, karbor, cullawine, colo, koala wombat, and New Holland sloth. Koala is a word from the Australian Aborigines that means "no drink." This is just the right name for this animal because it rarely drinks water.

The koala gets its liquid from the leaves of the eucalyptus trees. These leaves are almost the only food it will eat. Some koalas will eat only a certain type of eucalyptus leaf!

Write the many names the koala has been called in alphabetical order.

New Holland sloth      1. _____

koolewong               2. _____

colo                    3. _____

narnagoon               4. _____

karbor                  5. _____

bangaroo                6. _____

koala wombat            7. _____

native bear             8. _____

buidelbeer              9. _____

cullawine              10. _____

Unscramble the letters to write the missing words.

1.  The Aborigine word for "no drink" is _____.
    (o l k a a)

2.  Koalas eat only _____ of the
    (a v l e e s)

    _____ tree.
    (c s u p e y a t l u)

3.  A koala has thick gray _____, _____
    (r u f)            (u n r d o)

    ears, and a _____ _____.
    (b u s b t y)        (l a i t)

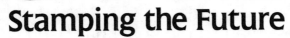

# Stamping the Future

Did you know that a stamp decided where a canal would be built? The people who were going to build the canal could not decide whether to build it in Panama or Nicaragua.

In 1900 a stamp was made with a picture of Mount Momotombo in Nicaragua on it. This was a dead volcano. But the picture showed the mountain erupting with fire and ash going everywhere.

When the builders saw the stamp, they began to worry. They wondered if maybe the mountain was not dead and that it just might erupt. They made their decision. Four years later the canal was built. Today many ships sail through the *Panama Canal*.

Mount Momotombo

Read each sentence. Look at the two stamps. Write the answer on the line.

1. If Mr. Rider wants to build an amusement park with a ferris wheel and rollercoaster, he would probably build it in _____.

2. If Ms. Homebody wants to build many new houses, she will probably build them in _____.

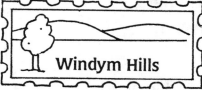
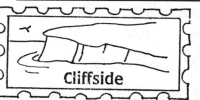

3. If Mr. Roadster is going to build many new roads, he will probably build them in _____.

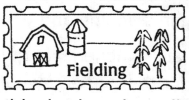

4. If Ms. Waterway is going to build a bridge, she will probably build it in _____.

# Into the Wastebasket

Plop! Gary threw another wadded sheet of paper into the wastebasket. He stared out the window. He had to write a story. What could he write?

Just then a tiny spider walked across his desk. Gary watched as the spider spun a thread to lower itself to the floor. Getting on his hands and knees, Gary followed the spider as it went under his bed.

The spider stopped, turned, and looked at Gary. It waited for Gary to follow. Then it walked to the corner. The spider slowly began spinning and weaving a thread.

Gary watched. He quietly crawled from under the bed and went back to his desk. Taking a sheet of paper from his notebook, he began to write his story.

Write what you think Gary wrote about in his story.

_____

_____

_____

_____

_____

_____

_____

_____

Draw a picture to show what you think the spider made while spinning and weaving a thread.

# Brush!

"Brush your teeth," reminds your mother. Do you grab a "chew stick?" This is a twig with one soft, ragged end. It was used by the Egyptians about 5000 years ago.

Or, maybe you would like to use a toothbrush like that used in China about 500 years ago. It had a bamboo handle. The bristles came from the hairs on the back of hogs' necks.

Of course, you could use a more modern toothbrush. About 200 years ago people in Europe used toothpicks. These were made from brass or silver.

Since you probably don't have any of these, you grab your nylon toothbrush. This toothbrush has been around for about sixty years. Maybe you have one of the newer models—a cordless electric toothbrush. This is only about thirty years old.

So, brush up. Brush down. Brush back and forth. Be sure to floss. Maybe the toothbrush of the future will do all of this and even put toothpaste on the brush for you.

Toothbrushes have changed over time. Use the sample pictures to help you draw each toothbrush in its correct place along the timeline.

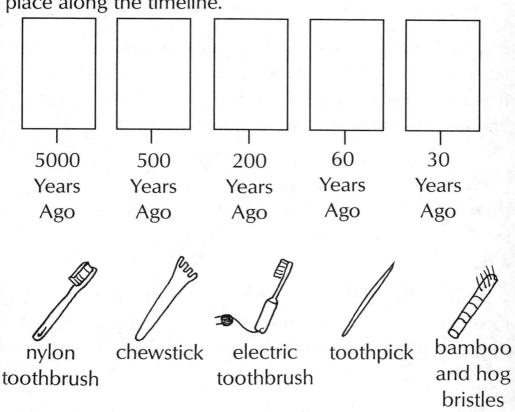

| 5000 Years Ago | 500 Years Ago | 200 Years Ago | 60 Years Ago | 30 Years Ago |

nylon toothbrush    chewstick    electric toothbrush    toothpick    bamboo and hog bristles

Draw a picture of a toothbrush of the future. Label the parts of the picture to tell what each will do.

# Doughnuts

There are many kinds of doughnuts. There are chocolate-covered, glazed, jelly-filled, and even applesauce-flavored. Buy one or buy a dozen. Doughnuts are fun and tasty to nibble just about any time of day.

The doughnut came to the United States with the Pilgrims. At that time it was called an oil cake because there was a lot of oil in the sweet dough. It was very small and round like a walnut. That is why it was called a *dough nut*.

Today's shape of doughnut was Hanson Gregory's idea. He poked holes in his mother's doughnuts so that they would fry more evenly and not be soggy in the middle.

Look closely at one of today's doughnut holes. Could it be the original dough nut?

Draw a line from each word or phrase on the bakery box to the correct doughnut picture(s).

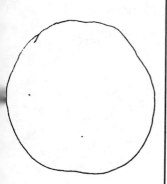

**Dough nut**

fries evenly

round

called oil cake

hole in middle

fried

eaten today

size of a walnut

sweet

soggy middle

eaten by Pilgrims

different flavors

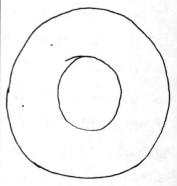

**American doughnut**

Write a description of your favorite kind of doughnut. Be sure to tell how it looks, smells, and tastes.

_____

_____

_____

_____

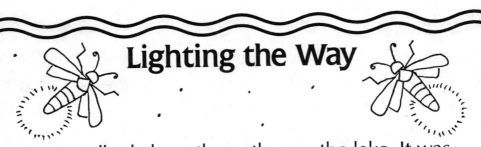

# Lighting the Way

Megan walked along the path near the lake. It was getting dark. She began walking back to where her family was camped. The tall trees cast shadows on the path. Megan had trouble seeing the way. She tripped on a rock.

Megan sat on the ground and rubbed her knee. Just then a tiny light flashed and then disappeared. She stood up and slowly walked along the trail. It was almost dark now.

Suddenly the tiny light appeared again. It was a firefly. Soon lots of tiny lights appeared. The fireflies moved close together. They made a big ball of bright light. Megan could easily see the path. She hurried along as the fireflies led the way.

When she reached her family, the fireflies scattered into dozens of tiny lights and flew off into the forest.

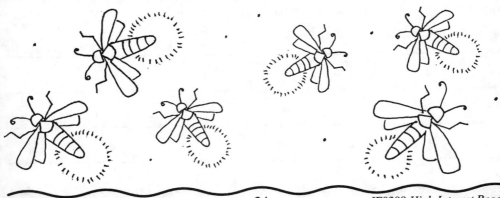

Read the words on the fireflies. Write the words in order to tell the main idea.

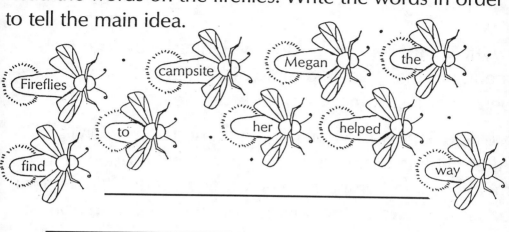

_____

_____

_____

Circle seven words in the puzzle that relate to fireflies.
They can go → ↓ .

| d | i | s | a | p | p | e | a | r | e | d |
|---|---|---|---|---|---|---|---|---|---|---|
| f | e | d | l | b | r | i | g | h | t | t |
| f | i | f | l | a | s | h | e | d | i | i |
| l | a | p | p | e | a | r | e | d | r | n |
| e | s | r | s | f | e | n | e | a | c | y |
| w | i | s | c | a | t | t | e | r | e | d |

This story is probably    fact

fiction

# Uncle Sam

Uncle Sam is a symbol for the United States government. For many years people didn't know if he was a real person or just someone's made-up idea.

Uncle Sam was a real person named Samuel Wilson. After fighting in the Revolutionary War, he opened a meat-packing company. Everyone called him Uncle Sam because he was a friendly person and a fair and honest businessman.

When Sam marked the crates of meat that were to be sold to the government, he just stamped them with the letters *US*.

Inspectors came to see the company. They asked a worker what the US meant. The worker didn't really know. As a joke, he said they were the initials of his boss—Uncle Sam.

The newspaper story that told about Sam Wilson and the letters *US* was not discovered for many years. About two hundred years after this event, the Congress of the United States officially stated that Samuel Wilson was the originator of our national symbol of Uncle Sam.

# Answer Key

## High-Interest Reading—Grade 2

---

**Page 5**

---

**Page 7**

1. Sail south to the two rocks.
2. Go east between the two rocks.
3. Steer north under the bridge.
4. Continue northwest to the Coast Guard Station.
5. Head north again to the Fishing Trips Office.
6. Slow the engines and go south toward the dock.
7. Go to slot C. Draw a picture of the boat.

---

**Page 9**

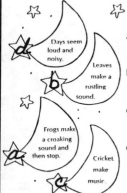

Days seem loud and noisy.

Leaves make a rustling sound.

Frogs make a croaking sound and then stop.

Cricket make music.

a. They are trying to find other frogs.

b. The wind blows through the branches.

c. They are rubbing their wings together.

d. There are lots of people and cars on the streets.

List the sounds you hear at night and tell what makes those sounds.

*Answers will vary.*

---

**Page 11**

1. Draw a picture of Cecil or Cindy.

*Picture should represent a centipede.*

2. What clue(s) in the story tell you about Cecil and Cindy?

*Tied lace #21 to lace #22*
*Tied sneaker #100*
*Raced to a leaf on a pumpkin plant*

Circle the answer.

1. What did Cecil and Cindy like to do?

 tease each other   (race)   tie their shoes

2. How many races did they have in the story?

 one   (two)   three   four

Write about another race Cecil and Cindy could have.

*Answers will vary.*

---

## Page 13

Follow the directions to make a beautiful fireworks display.

1. Connect the dots from a to r to make the shape of the fireworks.

2. Draw 5 yellow stars above the top point.

3. Draw 6 stripes on the top part of the fireworks. Color 3 stripes purple and 3 stripes orange.

4. Use three different colors to draw 9 wavy lines across the middle of the fireworks.

5. Color 2 of the flames orange and 3 flames red.

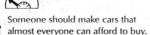

*Draw 5 yellow stars here.*

## Page 15

Read the clues. Find the correct word in the story and write it on the lines.

1. huge — g i g a n t i c
2. stood very still — f r o z e
3. part of the face — m o u t h
4. a forest animal — m o o s e
5. type of plants — f l o w e r s
6. opened and closed eyes — b l i n k e d
7. opposite of loudly — q u i e t l y
8. leaned — t i l t e d

Use the numbered letters to find out why Mom was so surprised that the moose ate her flowers.

Didn't the moose know that they were

t o u c h - m e -
n o t s?

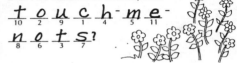

## Page 17

Read each sentence. Color the Full gas gauge if it is a good idea. Color the Empty gas gauge if it is a bad idea.

Empty / [Full filled] — Someone should make cars that almost everyone can afford to buy.

[Empty filled] / Full — We should be able to eat car parts.

*either* Empty / Full — Everyone should eat soybeans three times a day.

Empty / [filled] — Someone should find more uses for soybean oil.

Empty / [filled] — People should grow soybeans on every farm because there are so many uses for them.

Drawings will vary.

## Page 19

Andy's and Claire's
Answers will vary.

## Page 21

Check the correct box to tell when the words best describe Bumpler.

| | Before meeting Dr. Beeline | After meeting Dr. Beeline |
|---|---|---|
| unhappy | ✓ | |
| confident | | ✓ |
| embarrassed | ✓ | |
| poor vision | ✓ | |
| good vision | | ✓ |
| happy | | ✓ |
| clumsy | ✓ | |
| avoided things | | ✓ |
| liked buzzing around | | ✓ |

What name do you think his friends called him now?

*Answers will vary.*

Draw a picture of how Bumpler looks and feels at the end of the story.

*Drawings should depict Bumpler as happy and wearing glasses.*

## Page 23

Unscramble the letters and write the missing words on the lines.

1. From space the **Great Wall** looks like a thin **line**.
   (e a G t r) (l a l W) (in l e)
2. It is in northern **China**.
   (a n C i h)
3. It was built to **protect** China from its enemies.
   (t e p o r c t)
4. It took **hundreds** of years for the people to build the wall.
   (e h r u d n d s)
5. Only one **company** can sell pebbles from parts of the wall that have crumbled.
   (m c o p h a y)

Use the numbered letters to "build" the coded message.

**It is a truly "Great" Wall!**

## Page 25

Write the many names the koala has been called in alphabetical order.

| | | |
|---|---|---|
| New Holland sloth | 1. | bangaroo |
| koolewong | 2. | buidelbeer |
| colo | 3. | colo |
| narnagoon | 4. | cullawine |
| karbor | 5. | karbor |
| bangaroo | 6. | koala wombat |
| koala wombat | 7. | koolewong |
| native bear | 8. | narnagoon |
| buidelbeer | 9. | native bear |
| cullawine | 10. | New Holland sloth |

Unscramble the letters to write the missing words.

1. The Aborigine word for "no drink" is **koala**.
   (o l k a a)
2. Koalas eat only **leaves** of the **eucalyptus** tree.
   (a y l e e s) (c s u p e y a t l u)
3. A koala has thick gray **fur**, **round** ears, and a **stubby tail**.
   (r u f) (u n r d o) (b u s b t y) (l a i t)

## Page 27

Read each sentence. Look at the two stamps. Write the answer on the line. *Answers may vary.*

1. If Mr. Rider wants to build an amusement park with a ferris wheel and rollercoaster, he would probably build it in **Pleasantville**.

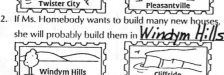
Twister City | Pleasantville

2. If Ms. Homebody wants to build many new houses, she will probably build them in **Windym Hills**.

Windym Hills | Cliffside

3. If Mr. Roadster is going to build many new roads, he will probably build them in **Metroburg**.

Metroburg | Fielding

4. If Ms. Waterway is going to build a bridge, she will probably build it in **River City**.

Dryhill | River City

## Page 29

Answers and pictures will vary.

## Page 31

Toothbrushes have changed over time. Use the sample pictures to help you draw each toothbrush in its correct place along the timeline.

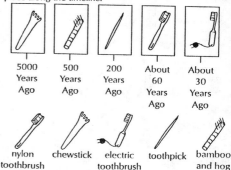

| 5000 Years Ago | 500 Years Ago | 200 Years Ago | About 60 Years Ago | About 30 Years Ago |
|---|---|---|---|---|

nylon toothbrush | chewstick | electric toothbrush | toothpick | bamboo and hog bristles

Draw a picture of a toothbrush of the future. Label the parts of the picture to tell what each will do.

Pictures will vary.

## Page 33

Draw a line from each word or phrase on the bakery box to the correct doughnut picture(s).

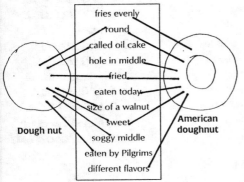

fries evenly
round
called oil cake
hole in middle
fried
eaten today
size of a walnut
sweet
soggy middle
eaten by Pilgrims
different flavors

**Dough nut**

**American doughnut**

Write a description of your favorite kind of doughnut. Be sure to tell how it looks, smells, and tastes.

_Descriptions will vary._

## Page 35

Read the words on the fireflies. Write the words in order to tell the main idea.

Fireflies · campsite · Megan · the · to · her · helped · find · way

_Fireflies helped Megan find her way to the campsite._

Circle seven words in the puzzle that relate to fireflies. They can go → ↓.

| d | i | s | a | p | p | e | a | r | e | d |
|---|---|---|---|---|---|---|---|---|---|---|
| f | e | d | l | b | r | i | g | h | t | t |
| l | i | f | l | a | s | h | e | d | i | i |
| l | a | p | p | e | a | r | e | d | r | n |
| e | s | r | s | f | e | n | e | a | c | y |
| w | i | s | c | a | t | t | e | r | e | d |

This story is probably (fiction) / fact

## Page 37

The sentence on the flag tells something that happened. Draw a line to the sentence on the star that tells why it happened.

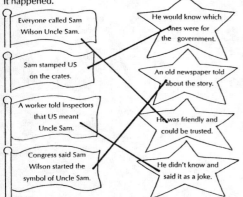

Everyone called Sam Wilson Uncle Sam.

Sam stamped US on the crates.

A worker told inspectors that US meant Uncle Sam.

Congress said Sam Wilson started the symbol of Uncle Sam.

He would know which ones were for the government.

An old newspaper told about the story.

He was friendly and could be trusted.

He didn't know and said it as a joke.

Today, two letters are used by the post office to represent each state. Find the correct letters in the State Bank and write them next to the name of each state.

| State Bank | | |
|---|---|---|
| MN | AL | OH |
| VT | OR | MI |
| NV | FL | CA |

Michigan **MI**   Minnesota **MN**
Ohio **OH**   Florida **FL**
Vermont **VT**   Alabama **AL**

## Page 39

Read the clues. Find the words in the story and write them in the puzzle.

1. opposite of dark
2. egg-shaped
3. misty end of a comet
4. ball of light with a tail

light
oval
tail
comet
orbet
astronomer
planet
telescope

5. a path around the sun
6. person who studies things in space
7. Earth is one
8. instrument used to look into space

Write the letters in the bold squares to find the name of the most recently discovered comet.

_Hale-Bopp_

Write the name you would give a comet that you discovered. _Answers will vary._

## Page 41

Read each sentence. If it tells something that could really happen, color the Frisbee yellow. If it tells something that is make-believe, color the Frisbee blue.

**yellow**
Wind can blow a Frisbee away from a dog.

**yellow**
A Frisbee rolls across the sand.

**blue**
A Frisbee can wave good-bye.

**yellow**
A dog can have big teeth and a mean growl.

**blue**
A Frisbee can roll defensively.

**yellow**
A family can play catch with a Frisbee.

**blue**
Frisbees can make new friends every day.

**blue**
A Frisbee can steer itself around a log.

Write about another new friend Freddie Frisbee meets on the beach.

_Answers will vary._

## Page 43

Write words that describe only a crocodile on the crocodile. Write words that describe only an alligator on the alligator. Write words that describe both reptiles on the fish.

_Possible Answers_

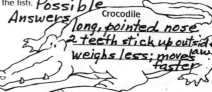

**Crocodile**
long, pointed nose
2 teeth stick up outside jaw
weighs less; moves faster

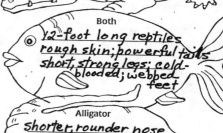

**Both**
12-foot long reptiles
rough skin; powerful tails
short, strong legs; cold-blooded; webbed feet

**Alligator**
shorter, rounder nose
no teeth seen when jaw closed
weighs more; moves slower

## Page 45

Number the sentences in the correct order to tell how you use a zipper to zip up a jacket. Use the picture to help you.

teeth

slide

holder

tab

**2** Slip the tab into the slide and holder.

**4** Move the slide up.

**1** Place the slide at the bottom into the holder.

**3** Hold the bottom ends together.

Today's zippers are used on suitcases, purses, dresses, jackets, pencil boxes, backpacks, spacesuits, and even tents.

Write the objects above in order from largest object to smallest.

_Answers may vary._

1. tents
2. suitcases
3. spacesuits
4. dresses
5. jackets
6. backpacks
7. purses
8. pencil boxes

## Page 47

Color the pillow that tells the main idea, **blue.** Color the other pillows **yellow.**

**yellow**
Moms always tell kids to make their beds.

**blue**
Beds are easier and quicker to make today.

**yellow**
Beds need to be made.

**yellow**
Everyone likes a neatly made bed.

**yellow**
There are all kinds of beds.

| Word Bank | Find and circle the words in the puzzle ( → ↓ ). |
|---|---|
| sheets | |
| sack | |
| straw | |
| smooth | |
| bench | |
| blankets | |
| bedspread | |
| rough | |
| floor | |
| pillow | |
| stuff | |
| easy | |
| table | |

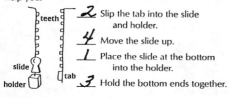

## Page 49

Read and follow the directions. Draw a line to show where the honeyguide leads the badger to find the beehive.

1. Start at the honeyguide.
2. Go right 5 spaces. Draw a bush in this space.
3. Now go down 2 spaces. Draw a giraffe in this space.
4. Go left 4 spaces. Draw an elephant.
5. Then go down 3 spaces. Draw a zebra.
6. Go right 5 spaces. Draw a river.
7. Now go up 2 spaces. Draw a lion.
8. Go left 3 spaces. Draw a monkey.
9. Go down 1 space. Draw a beehive.

## Page 51

Read each sentence. If it describes Rosie, write **R** in the toy mouse. If it describes Sylvester, write **S** in the toy mouse.

1. This one teased others. *S*

2. This one kept getting into trouble. *R*

3. This one was sneaky. *S*

4. This one tried to behave. *R*

5. This one got angry. *R*

6. This one liked to get others in trouble. *S*

7. This one finally behaved. *S*

8. This one told the truth. *R*

Draw a picture of Rosie's family photo.

*4 cats — Mom, Dad, Sylvester, Rosie*

## Page 53

The sentence on each train engine tells something that happened. Find the sentence that tells why it happened and write the letter on the train's smokestack.

*c* Ching Su wanted to work on building the railroad.

a. The ship would sail to California.

*a* He boarded a ship in Hong Kong.

b. His hard work had earned him a lot of money and the respect of others.

*d* Ching Su cut trees, crushed rock, raked the ground, and pounded spikes.

c. He could earn $28.00 a month.

*b* Ching Su felt very proud.

d. The ground had to be level for the railroad track.

Why was the railroad so important?

*It connected the eastern and western sections of U.S.*

Write about something you did that made you feel very proud of yourself. *Answers will vary.*

## Page 55

Color the fern **green** if the words tell something the characters did in the story. Color the fern **brown** if they did not do it.

*green* watered the plants

*brown* cut down trees

*green* planted ferns

*green* hauled dirt

*green* raked

*brown* planted three trees

*green* worked hard

*green* planted flowers

*green* planted two trees

Draw and color a picture that shows how the backyard looked at the end of the story. Be sure to include everything they bought.

*Pictures will vary.*

## Page 57

The sentence on the bowl tells something that happened. Draw a line to the sentence on the peanut that tells why it happened.

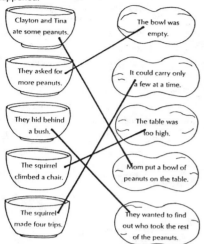

Clayton and Tina ate some peanuts.

The bowl was empty.

They asked for more peanuts.

It could carry only a few at a time.

They hid behind a bush.

The table was too high.

The squirrel climbed a chair.

Mom put a bowl of peanuts on the table.

The squirrel made four trips.

They wanted to find out who took the rest of the peanuts.

Why do you think the squirrel took all of the peanuts?

*To store them to eat later.*

## Page 59

Read the clues. Write the words from the story in the puzzle.

```
¹c h u b b y
  t h i n
²p a t r i o t i c
        f l a g
        b e a r d
    s t r i p e s
        s t a r s
        s y m b o l s
```

1. The first Uncle Sam was drawn short and _____ .
2. After the Civil War, he was drawn tall and _____ .
3. Artists thought Uncle Sam should look more _____ .
4. There are stars and stripes on the United States _____ .
5. Uncle Sam was drawn with a _____ when Abe Lincoln was president.
6. Today his pants have red and white _____ .
7. His hat now has white _____ on it.
8. Stars and stripes are _____ on the U.S. flag.

Write the letters in the highlighted squares in order to see whose name appears. *Uncle Sam*

## Page 61

Draw a line on the map to show the path the character had to walk to get to school today. Use a green crayon to show the path the character usually walked to get to school.

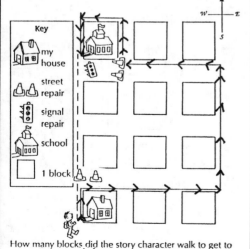

Key

🏠 my house

street repair

signal repair

🏫 school

1 block

How many blocks did the story character walk to get to school today? __11__

## Page 63

**Across**

2. A poorwill _____ in winter.

3. The temperature of its body falls ___ normal.

4. There is almost no _____ .

7. It burrows among the _____ .

**Down**

1. A poorwill does not migrate in ___ .
2. The Hopi name for this bird is ___ .
5. It _____ in an opening in the rocks.
6. It _____ when the snow melts.

```
        w
        i
        n
²h i b e r n a t e s
  o     e
¹b e l o w        ²
  c
  k  ³h e a r t b e a t
  ¹r o c k s  u  w
        r  a
        r  k
        o  e
        w  n
        s  s
```

## Page 65

Draw a  above the words that describe the mouse.

Draw an [house icon] above the words that describe the owner.

[muffin icon] kind    [muffin icon] frightened    [muffin icon] keeps trying

[muffin icon] hungry    [house icon] gentle    [muffin+house icon] happy

Why was the mouse a perfect mascot for the Muffin Bakery?

*The owner's last name was Mouse.*
*The mouse liked to eat muffins.*

Draw a picture of a sign that might be used for the bakery. Be sure to include the name of the bakery.

*Signs will vary.*

## Page 67

Draw a ( ) around the correct answers.

1. What did Terry read on the label?
   Animal Cooky Company    **(Baker's Magic Cookie Company)**    Forest Cookie Company

2. Where do a bear, moose, and squirrel live?
   ocean    jungle    **(forest)**    zoo    farm

3. Which other animal shapes might the moose cookie cutter make?
   elephant    **(deer)**    penguin    **(chipmunk)**

4. If this cookie company made a balloon-shaped cookie cutter, then it would probably make shapes of things at... a hospital.    **(a circus.)**

5. If this cookie company made a jellyfish-shaped cookie cutter, then it would probably make shapes of... **(animals in the sea.)**    animals in a jungle.

6. If this cookie company made a pencil-shaped cookie cutter, then it would probably make shapes of...
   **(things used in school.)**    things used in a kitchen.

7. If this cookie company made a carrot-shaped cookie cutter, then it would probably make shapes of... **(vegetables.)**    fruits.

## Page 69

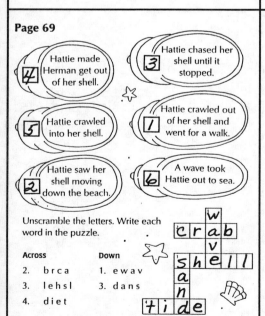

[4] Hattie made Herman get out of her shell.
[3] Hattie chased her shell until it stopped.
[5] Hattie crawled into her shell.
[1] Hattie crawled out of her shell and went for a walk.
[2] Hattie saw her shell moving down the beach.
[6] A wave took Hattie out to sea.

Unscramble the letters. Write each word in the puzzle.

**Across**
2. brca
3. lehsl
4. diet

**Down**
1. ewav
3. dans

crab / wave / shell / sand / tide

## Page 71

Answers will vary.

## Page 72

Visit the animals that live in the wild. Use the Word Bank to write the name of each animal that fits in the puzzle.

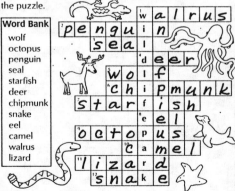

**Word Bank**
wolf
octopus
penguin
seal
starfish
deer
chipmunk
snake
eel
camel
walrus
lizard

walrus / penguin / seal / deer / wolf / chipmunk / starfish / eel / octopus / camel / lizard / snake

The Wildlife Park has 4 animal areas:
Forest    Sea    Arctic    Desert

Write in which area of the park you will see the animals.

Animals #1–3: *Arctic*    Animals #4–6: *Forest*
Animals #7–9: *Sea*    Animals #10–12: *Desert*

The sentence on the flag tells something that happened. Draw a line to the sentence on the star that tells why it happened.

**Flags:**
- Everyone called Sam Wilson Uncle Sam.
- Sam stamped US on the crates.
- A worker told inspectors that US meant Uncle Sam.
- Congress said Sam Wilson started the symbol of Uncle Sam.

**Stars:**
- He would know which ones were for the government.
- An old newspaper told about the story.
- He was friendly and could be trusted.
- He didn't know and said it as a joke.

Today, two letters are used by the post office to represent each state. Find the correct letters in the State Bank and write them next to the name of each state.

| State Bank | | |
|---|---|---|
| MN | AL | OH |
| VT | OR | MI |
| NV | FL | CA |

Michigan ____   Minnesota ____

Ohio ____   Florida ____

Vermont ____   Alabama ____

# Comet Sense

Look! Over there! It's a bright ball of light connected to a misty-like stream. It's a comet! Is it one that astronomers already know about? Or is it a new one that no one has seen before?

Over the years scientists have drawn maps of the sky. When something new appears, they look at their maps and compare what they know is there with what is new in the sky.

Just as our planet and the other eight planets travel in an orbit (or path) around the sun, so do comets. A comet's orbit is oval or egg-shaped, rather than round like a planet's orbit.

We can see comets without a telescope only when they travel close to the sun. The comet's tail of dust, ice, metal, and rocky particles make a trail behind the ball when it gets near the sun. After the comet goes around the sun and heads back out into space, the tail is in front of the ball. It makes a spectacular sight!

Read the clues. Find the words in the story and write them in the puzzle.

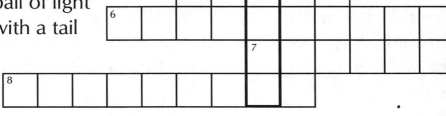

1. opposite of dark
2. egg-shaped
3. misty end of a comet
4. ball of light with a tail

5. a path around the sun
6. person who studies things in space
7. Earth is one
8. instrument used to look into space

Write the letters in the bold squares to find the name of the most recently discovered comet.

_____

Write the name you would give a comet that you

discovered. _____

# Free-Wheeling Freddie

"Hey! Wait! You forgot me!" thought Freddie the Frisbee. "I guess I'll just lie in the sand for a while."

Whoosh! A strong wind gust lifted Freddie on his side. He rolled along the sand.

"Whew! That was close," sighed Freddie as he leaned to avoid some driftwood. "This beach calls for defensive rolling."

Freddie rolled near a boy and his dog. The dog growled. "My, what big teeth you have," cringed Freddie. The wind quickly blew him away from the dog's grasping teeth.

Then Freddie rolled near a boy and girl. The girl picked him up and tossed him to her brother. Soon Mom and Dad joined the game. Freddie thought this was great fun. Then it was time for the family to leave. The girl set Freddie on his side. The wind pushed him along the sand. The children waved and called out, "Have fun with new friends tomorrow!" Freddie leaned from side to side as he waved good-bye.

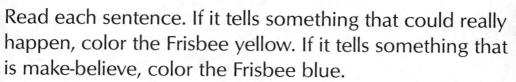

Read each sentence. If it tells something that could really happen, color the Frisbee yellow. If it tells something that is make-believe, color the Frisbee blue.

Wind can blow a Frisbee away from a dog.

A Frisbee rolls across the sand.

A Frisbee can wave good-bye.

A dog can have big teeth and a mean growl.

A Frisbee can roll defensively.

A family can play catch with a Frisbee.

Frisbees can make new friends every day.

A Frisbee can steer itself around a log.

Write about another new friend Freddie the Frisbee meets on the beach.

_____

_____

_____

# Reptile Relatives

Do you know the difference between crocodiles and alligators? Look closely.

Both are twelve feet long. Rough skin covers their bodies from their heads to the tips of their powerful tails. Their legs are short but very strong.

While warming their cold-blooded bodies in the sun, each yawns and then snaps its mouth shut. On each side of the crocodile's long, pointed nose a sharp tooth sticks up outside its lower jaw. The alligator with its shorter, rounder nose closes its mouth. No teeth can be seen.

Both reptiles have webbed feet. Weighing less than the alligator, the crocodile can move faster.

Write words that describe only a crocodile on the crocodile. Write words that describe only an alligator on the alligator. Write words that describe both reptiles on the fish.

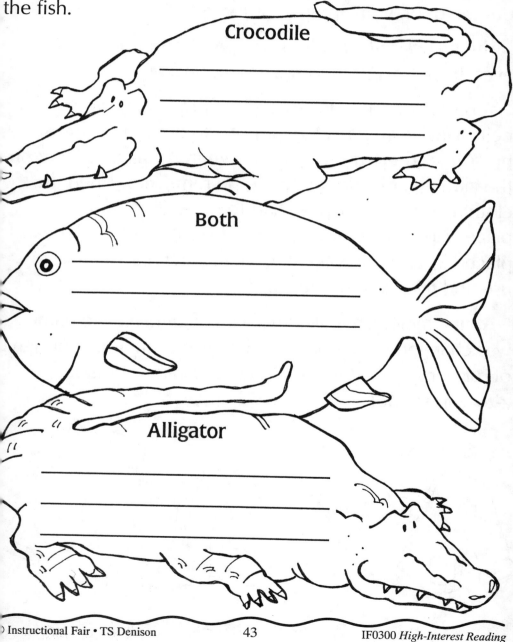

**Crocodile**

**Both**

**Alligator**

# Zip!

Each school morning you unzip your backpack, stuff in whatever you need, and zip it closed. Then, as you rush out the door, you zip up your jacket.

The first *clasp-locker* looked like rows of hooks and eyes. It was invented to replace shoelaces.

Today's design was first used on boots and money belts. Finally *zippers* were put on clothes. There were problems. They rusted quickly. When it was time to wash the clothing, the zipper had to be removed. When the clothing dried, the zipper had to be sewn back into place. Zippers were such a new idea that a booklet was placed in each package. It gave instructions on how to use and take care of the zipper.

At first they were called *hookless fasteners*. The name was changed to zipper when it was put on a new design of rubber boot. When it was being closed, it made a z-z-z-z-ip sound!

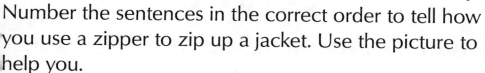

Number the sentences in the correct order to tell how you use a zipper to zip up a jacket. Use the picture to help you.

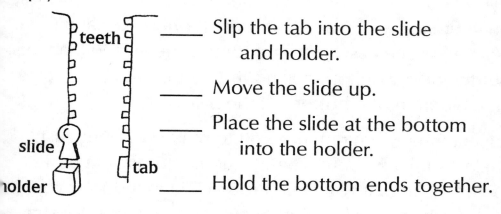

_____ Slip the tab into the slide and holder.

_____ Move the slide up.

_____ Place the slide at the bottom into the holder.

_____ Hold the bottom ends together.

Today's zippers are used on suitcases, purses, dresses, jackets, pencil boxes, backpacks, spacesuits, and even tents.

Write the objects above in order from largest object to smallest .

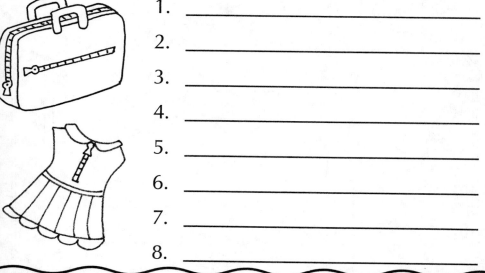

1. _____

2. _____

3. _____

4. _____

5. _____

6. _____

7. _____

8. _____

# "Aw, Mom!"

At least once a week you hear Mom say, "Be sure to make your bed." With a wrinkled nose and grumpy look on your face, you make your bed. It only takes a minute. It's really quite easy. Just smooth the sheets and blankets, put the pillow on top, pull up the bedspread, and tuck a little bit under the bottom of the pillow. You're finished!

Next time Mom reminds you to make your bed just smile and think about what it was like to make a bed long, long ago. If you were lucky to sleep indoors, you had to *make your bed*. You would grab handfuls of straw and stuff them into a sack made of rough cloth. Then you would put it on a bench, table, or the floor. This was your bed. You hoped to have a blanket to wrap around you on a cold night. In the morning you would dump the straw out of the sack. Then at night you had to "make your bed" again.

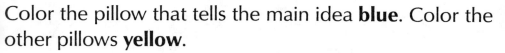

Color the pillow that tells the main idea **blue**. Color the other pillows **yellow**.

Moms always tell kids to make their beds.

Beds are easier and quicker to make today.

Beds need to be made.

Everyone likes a neatly made bed.

There are all kinds of beds.

**Word Bank**

sheets
sack
straw
smooth
bench
blankets
bedspread
rough
floor
pillow
stuff
easy
table

Find and circle the words in the puzzle ( →↓ ).

| b | a | a | l | s | t | r | a | w | e | e | s |
|---|---|---|---|---|---|---|---|---|---|---|---|
| e | s | d | f | c | y | e | b | e | n | c | h |
| d | h | t | l | u | i | t | e | a | o | p | m |
| s | e | r | o | b | l | a | n | k | e | t | s |
| p | e | k | o | c | q | y | u | e | l | a | i |
| r | t | a | r | o | d | d | l | o | o | g | e |
| e | s | m | p | i | l | l | o | w | y | n | a |
| a | b | r | n | k | s | t | u | f | f | r | s |
| d | a | t | a | b | l | e | n | o | l | d | y |
| s | a | t | e | e | s | m | o | o | t | h | a |
| t | s | a | c | k | m | r | o | u | g | h | t |

# Honey of a Guide

Spread some honey on a slice of warm bread. Yum! What a great sweet treat!

Animals like honey, too. In Africa and southern Asia there are small birds called honeyguides. They like to eat the wax of a honeycomb. But for them to get to the wax in a honeycomb, another animal must first break it open. Since hives cannot always be easily found, the honeyguide must lead another animal to the hive.

When the honeyguide finds a beehive, it chirps and fans its tail to get the attention of a honey badger. This animal likes honey, so he follows the honeyguide. When the honey badger reaches the hive, he breaks it open and eats the honey. After the honey badger has finished eating, the honeyguide then enjoys eating the wax. These two animals certainly make a "honey" of a pair.

Follow the directions. Draw a line to show where the honeyguide leads the honey badger to find the beehive.

1. Start at the honeyguide.
2. Go right 5 spaces. Draw a bush in this space.
3. Now go down 2 spaces. Draw a giraffe in this space.
4. Go left 4 spaces. Draw an elephant.
5. Then go down 3 spaces. Draw a zebra.
6. Go right 5 spaces. Draw a river.
7. Now go up 2 spaces. Draw a lion.
8. Go left 3 spaces. Draw a monkey.
9. Go down 1 space. Draw a beehive.

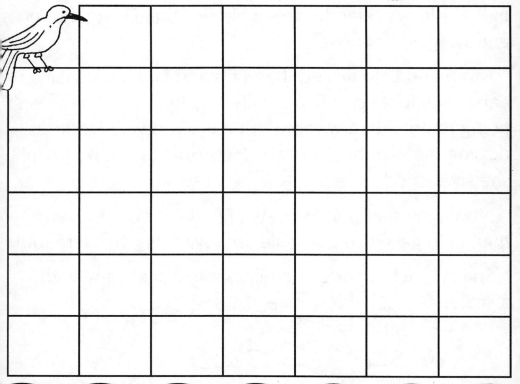

# The Family Photo

Mom, Dad, Sylvester, and Rosie sat very still. Amy wanted to take their picture. Sylvester turned his head just as Amy said, "Catnip." His whiskers touched Rosie's nose. She sneezed.

"Okay," said Amy with a sigh. "Let's try this again."

Sylvester yawned. His whiskers tickled Rosie's ear. She shook her head.

"Now sit still, please," begged Amy.

Mom and Dad gave Rosie a stern look. They smiled at Sylvester. He lifted his head and purred, "Na-na-na-nana." His whiskers tickled Rosie's whiskers. She closed her eyes and wiggled her nose.

Mom and Dad flicked their tails and laid back their ears. They looked at Rosie with very big eyes. She wasn't going to get into any more trouble. "Yeow! Sylvester is tickling me with his whiskers. He's doing it on purpose!" she screeched.

Now they stared at Sylvester. Dad moved between them. He gave Rosie a smile and Sylvester the stern look.

Snap! "Such a perfect family photo," said Amy with a smile.

Read each sentence. If it describes Rosie, write **R** in
the toy mouse. If it describes Sylvester, write **S** in the
toy mouse.

1. This one teased others.

2. This one kept getting
   into trouble.

3. This one was sneaky.

4. This one tried to behave.

5. This one got angry.

6. This one liked to get others
   in trouble.

7. This one finally behaved.

8. This one told the truth.

Draw a picture of Rosie's
family photo.

# Job Well Done

One day in a small Chinese village Ching Su read an ad asking for workers to build a railroad in the United States. The ad said workers could earn $28.00 in a month. Ching Su worked hard to earn just $3.00 in a month.

Boarding a ship in Hong Kong, he sailed for California. When he landed, he rode in a wagon to the end of the railroad track. The next morning he began working. Ching Su used a pick and shovel to cut out tree stumps and break up large rocks. Then he loaded the stumps and crushed rock into carts. He raked the roadbed to make it smooth and level. When the railroad ties were laid down, he pounded the large spikes to keep the rails in place. Day after day, he worked very hard.

When the last spike was pounded into the rail, Ching Su stood proudly. He had earned a large wage and the respect of the railroad owners. Ching Su had been a part of history—connecting the western and eastern parts of the United States.

The sentence on each train engine tells something that happened. Find the sentence that tells why it happened and write the letter on the train's smokestack.

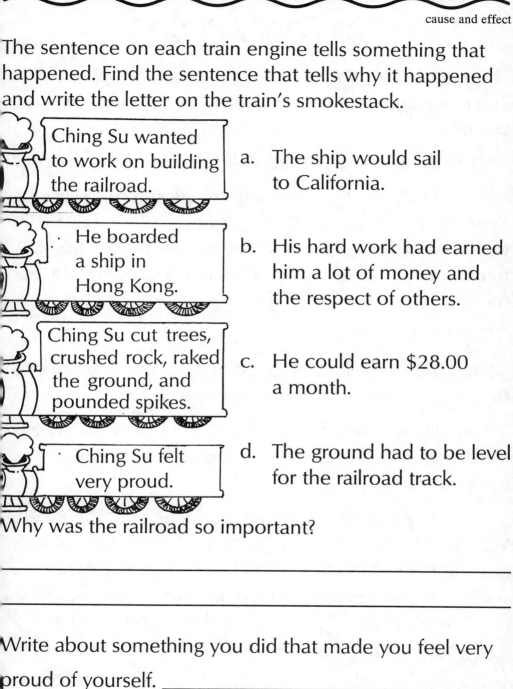

Ching Su wanted to work on building the railroad.

a. The ship would sail to California.

He boarded a ship in Hong Kong.

b. His hard work had earned him a lot of money and the respect of others.

Ching Su cut trees, crushed rock, raked the ground, and pounded spikes.

c. He could earn $28.00 a month.

Ching Su felt very proud.

d. The ground had to be level for the railroad track.

Why was the railroad so important?

_____

_____

Write about something you did that made you feel very proud of yourself. _____

_____

# The Family Project

One Saturday morning Dad looked at the backyard. The fence and deck looked great. The yard looked horrible.

"Hmmmm," thought Dad. "I know what we can do."

Mitzi, Dad, and I jumped into the pickup truck. We drove to the Garden of Dreams Nursery. It was filled with rows of beautiful trees and plants. I looked up at trees twice as tall as myself. They had lots of tiny leaves on their branches.

"Let's get this tree," I said.

"And this one," said Mitzi, pointing to another tall tree that was covered with tiny pink blossoms.

Carefully we loaded some ferns, some flowers, the two trees, and even a birdbath into the pickup. We drove back home.

We worked all day in the yard. We mowed. We raked. We dug. We hauled dirt in the wheelbarrow. We planted, and then we watered. At last we set the birdbath between the two trees. Very tired and very dirty, we looked at our day's project. Our backyard was now beautiful!

Color the fern **green** if the words tell something the characters did in the story. Color the fern **brown** if they did not do it.

watered the plants

cut down trees

planted ferns

hauled dirt

raked

planted three trees

worked hard

planted flowers

planted two trees

Draw and color a picture that shows how the backyard looked at the end of the story. Be sure to include everything they bought.

# The Mystery of the Vanishing Peanuts

Mom set a bowl of peanuts on the patio table. Clayton and Tina each ate a big handful. Then they ran out into the yard to play catch.

Soon they went back for more peanuts. "Hey, Mom!" they shouted. "May we have more peanuts?"

"How could you two eat that whole bowlful already?" she asked.

Clayton and Tina each took a few from the bowl. Then they set the bowl on the table. After that they hid behind a bush and quietly watched.

Soon a gray squirrel ran to the patio and climbed onto a chair. It stood on its hind legs. With its tiny paws, it reached into the bowl and quickly stuffed peanuts into its mouth. Then it scurried away. The little squirrel made four trips before it completely emptied the bowl.

"Well, that solved the mystery of the vanishing peanuts," laughed Tina. "Of course, now we need to ask Mom for another bowlful for us!"

The sentence on the bowl tells something that happened.
Draw a line to the sentence on the peanut that tells why
it happened.

Clayton and Tina ate some peanuts.

The bowl was empty.

They asked for more peanuts.

It could carry only a few at a time.

They hid behind a bush.

The table was too high.

The squirrel climbed a chair.

Mom put a bowl of peanuts on the table.

The squirrel made four trips.

They wanted to find out who took the rest of the peanuts.

Why do you think the squirrel took all of the peanuts?

# A Patriotic Picture

Uncle Sam was first drawn as a short, chubby man without a beard. He was dressed in a black top hat and black suit.

Later an artist made one change. He drew Uncle Sam wearing red pants. When Abraham Lincoln was president, one artist made another change. Uncle Sam was drawn with a beard. After the Civil War, an artist drew Uncle Sam as a tall, thin man.

Uncle Sam became such a favorite national symbol that artists decided that he should look more patriotic. Many changes were made. White stars and blue and white stripes were drawn on his top hat. His jacket became blue and his pants had red and white stripes. After many years and many artists, Uncle Sam became a truly patriotic character wearing the colors and symbols of the flag of the United States.

Read the clues. Write the words from the story in the puzzle.

1. The first Uncle Sam was drawn short and _____ .

2. After the Civil War, he was drawn tall and _____ .

3. Artists thought Uncle Sam should look more _____ .

4. There are stars and stripes on the United States _____ .

5. Uncle Sam was drawn with a _____ when Abe Lincoln was president.

6. Today his pants have red and white _____ .

7. His hat now has white _____ on it.

8. Stars and stripes are _____ on the U.S. flag.

Write the letters in the highlighted squares in order to see whose name appears. _____

# The Fortune Cookie

We finished eating our fried rice, sweet and sour pork, and chicken chow mein. The waiter brought the fortune cookies. We were all stuffed, but we each still took a cookie from the plate. I pulled out the paper strip. It said, "You will travel far." I laughed. "Sure, I will. I will travel all four blocks to school tomorrow!"

The next morning I grabbed my backpack and rushed out the door. I walked the first block to the corner. It was blocked off for street repair.

I turned right and walked three blocks before I could cross the street. After two blocks, I turned left. I walked two blocks. Again the street was blocked by a crew fixing the signal lights. I had to walk north one more block. At last I could cross the street. It was getting late so I ran the last block to the school.

The bell rang just as I sat down at my desk. "My fortune cookie was right!" I laughed.

Bring good luck!

Draw a line on the map to show the path the character had to walk to get to school today. Use a green crayon to show the path the character usually walked to get to school.

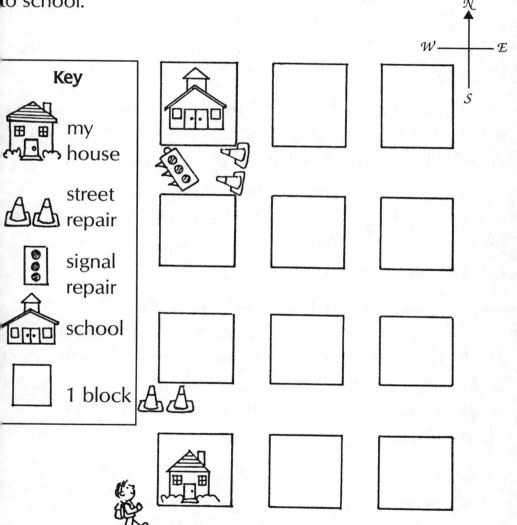

How many blocks did the story character walk to get to school today? _____

# Just a Seasonal Nap

It's getting colder. The leaves have changed color and are quickly falling to the ground. The birds are flying south for the winter. They want to be warm and able to find food.

But, not **all** birds migrate to the south. One called the poorwill hibernates—just like a bear! The Hopi Indians called this grayish-brown bird a *holchko* or "sleeper."

It burrows into a small opening in the rocks of the Sierra Nevada mountains and sleeps for the winter. Its body temperature drops below normal and there is hardly even a heartbeat.

When the snow melts, it awakens. It is healthy and weighs the same as it did before its "winter nap." Through spring, summer, and fall it enjoys building a nest gathering food and raising its family. But when the winter winds blow, the poorwill returns to its small opening in the mountainside to sleep.

Use the Word Bank and clues to complete the puzzle.

## Word Bank

| | | |
|---|---|---|
| awakens | below | hibernates |
| temperature | rocks | above |
| heartbeat | burrows | migrates |
| spring | winter | holchko |

## Across

2. A poorwill _____ in winter.

3. The temperature of its body falls ___ normal.

4. There is almost no _____ .

7. It burrows among the _____ .

## Down

1. A poorwill does not migrate in ____ .

2. The Hopi name for this bird is ____ .

5. It _____ in an opening in the rocks.

6. It _____ when the snow melts.

# Mike Mouse's Muffin Mascot

Mouse wiggled through the hole in the wall. Something smelled good. He climbed up on the counter. There were packages and packages of muffins. Mouse couldn't open the tough plastic with his tiny claws. He saw that one corner of a package was not pressed down. Curling his tiny claws under the loose edge, he used all his strength to lift it. 1 – 2 – 3 – lift! Oops! Mouse did a somersault. But he did get the package open.

Mouse nibbled on the muffin. Soon he was very full and very sleepy. He waddled over to a towel, curled up and went to sleep.

When the owner, Mike Mouse, came to work, he saw the little sleeping mouse and smiled. He got a big cage. Gently he put the sleeping mouse in it.

At last Mouse woke up. He was frightened. Then a smiling face looked into the cage. A soft voice said, "Good morning. I hope you like your new home. I've been looking for a mascot for my bakery. You're perfect! You even like my muffins!"

Draw a 🧁 above the words that describe the mouse.

Draw an 👕 above the words that describe the owner.

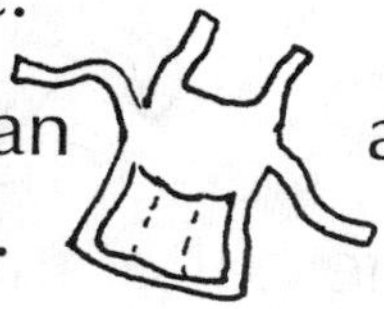

kind                    frightened              keeps trying

hungry                  gentle                  happy

Why was the mouse a perfect mascot for the Muffin Bakery?

_____

_____

_____

Draw a picture of a sign that might be used for the bakery. Be sure to include the name of the bakery.

# Curious Cookie Cutter

Terry pressed the moose-shaped cookie cutter into the dough. It made a perfect moose-shaped cookie. As he pressed the cookie cutter into the dough again, he thought about a bushy-tailed squirrel. This time the dough was cut into the shape of a squirrel. Terry looked at the cookie cutter. It **was** shaped like a moose!

Then he thought about a bear as he pressed the cutter into the dough. You guessed it! The dough was cut in the shape of a bear.

Terry read the label on the cookie cutter box. "Well, that explains it!" he said with a laugh.

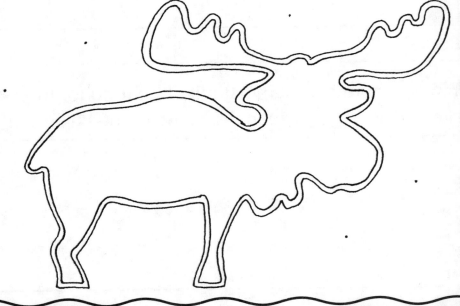

Draw a ◯ around the correct answers.

1. What did Terry read on the label?

   Animal Cooky Company    Baker's Magic Cookie Company    Forest Cookie Company

2. Where do a bear, moose, and squirrel live?

   ocean    jungle    forest    zoo    farm

3. Which other animal shapes might the moose cookie cutter make?

   elephant    deer    penguin    chipmunk

4. If this cookie company made a balloon-shaped cookie cutter, then it would probably make shapes of things at...    a hospital.    a circus.

5. If this cookie company made a jellyfish-shaped cookie cutter, then it would probably make shapes of...    animals in the sea.    animals in a jungle.

6. If this cookie company made a pencil-shaped cookie cutter, then it would probably make shapes of...

   things used in school.    things used in a kitchen.

7. If this cookie company made a carrot-shaped cookie cutter, then it would probably make shapes of...    vegetables.    fruits.

# Never Leave Home Without It

Hattie the Hermit Crab crawled out from her shell and went for a walk along the warm sand. When the tide began coming in, Hattie headed back toward her shell. But her shell was gone!

"There goes my shell!" she yelled. Quickly she caught up to her shell.

"Hey! You inside my shell! Stop!" she screamed.

It stopped. Out peeked a little crab face.

"Herman! I should have known," said Hattie disgustedly. "Go find your own shell!"

"But I did. I found your shell!" said Herman with a big grin.

"Out! Out! Out!" demanded Hattie.

"Okay, okay," answered Herman.

He wiggled out of the shell. Quickly Hattie crawled into her shell. She watched Herman walk down the beach.

"A crab should never leave home without its shell!" she said, as a wave gently lifted her.

ead the sentence on each shell. Number them in
ıe correct order by writing the number in the box
n the shell.

Hattie made
Herman get out
of her shell.

Hattie chased her
shell until it
stopped.

Hattie crawled
into her shell.

Hattie crawled out
of her shell and
went for a walk.

Hattie saw her
shell moving
down the beach.

A wave took
Hattie out to sea.

Jnscramble the letters. Write each
vord in the puzzle.

**cross**

. b r c a

. l e h s l

. d i e t

**Down**

1. e w a v

3. d a n s

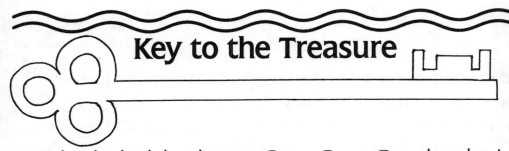

# Key to the Treasure

Dad unlocked the door to Great Great Grandmother's house. Sally and John rushed inside.

They raced up the stairs. John grabbed the knob on the railing. Oops! It came off the post. He stopped and went to put it back.

"Look at this, Sally," he said, as he waved for her to come back down the stairs. "This post is hollow. There's something down inside it."

Sally stuck her arm down inside the post. She pulled out a small velvet bag. There was a small key inside the bag.

"I wonder what it unlocks," said John.

Sally and John walked into the living room. On the wall over the fireplace was a picture of Great Great Grandmother.

"Look," whispered John. "She's holding this key in her hand."

"The key is pointing to that bookcase. Let's check the bookcase," said Sally excitedly.

"Wow! Look at...

Write what you think happened next.

_____

_____

_____

_____

_____

Draw a picture showing what the key unlocked and what
Sally and John found.

classificatic

# Visit the Wildlife

Visit the animals that live in the wild. Use the Word Bank to write the name of each animal that fits in the puzzle.

**Word Bank**

- wolf
- octopus
- penguin
- seal
- starfish
- deer
- chipmunk
- snake
- eel
- camel
- walrus
- lizard

1 **w**
2
3 **l**
4 **d**
5 **l**
6 **i**
7 **f**
8 **e**
  **p**
9
10 **a**
  **r**
11
12 **k**

The Wildlife Park has 4 animal areas:

Forest          Sea          Arctic          Desert

Write in which area of the park you will see the animals.

Animals #1–3: _____     Animals #4–6: _____

Animals #7–9: _____     Animals #10–12: _____